**OFFICIAL**

# DICK, KERR
## ·LADIES·

## FOOTBALL'S FORGOTTEN LEGENDS

### GAIL J. NEWSHAM

uclanpublishing

# CONTENTS

uclanpublishing

With thanks to Barney at Preston Digital Archive, Michael Barrett, Red Rose Collections and Harris Museum

*Dick, Kerr Ladies: Football's Forgotten Legends* is a uclanpublishing book

First published in Great Britain in 2021 by
uclanpublishing
University of Central Lancashire
Preston, PR1 2HE, UK

Text copyright © Gail J. Newsham, 2021
Illustration copyright © Thy Bui 2021

Designed by Amy Cooper
Edited by Emma Roberts

ISBN 978 1 912979 46 2

## Cover and interior illustrations by Thy Bui

IMAGE CREDITS IN ORDER OF APPEARANCE:
Key: t= top; m=middle; b=bottom; l=left; r=right

p3 t: Gail J. Newsham archive m: James Boyes b: Gail J. Newsham archive, p4 t: Théobald Chartran, Public domain, via Wikimedia Commons b: Shutterstock, p5 Gail J. Newsham archive, p6 t: Gail J. Newsham archive b: BAE Systems Heritage, Warton, p7 t: Courtesy of Lancashire County Council's Red Rose Collection and the estate of Mr C.R. Shaw, p8 Shutterstock, p9 t: Gail J. Newsham archive b: Harris Museum, Art Gallery & Library, Preston, England, p10 Eybl, Plakatmuseum Wien/Wikimedia Commons, p11 t & b: Gail J. Newsham archive, p12 t: Courtesy of Lancashire County Council's Red Rose Collection and the estate of Mr C.R. Shaw b: Shutterstock, p13 t: Preston Digital Archive b: Gail J. Newsham archive, p14 t: Courtesy of Lancashire County Council's Red Rose Collection and the estate of Mr C.R. Shaw, p15 t: Shutterstock b: Gail J. Newsham archive, p16-17 Gail J. Newsham archive, p19 l: Shutterstock r: Gail J. Newsham archive, p23 m: Preston Digital Archive b: Gail J. Newsham archive, p24-25 Shutterstock, p27-31 Gail J. Newsham archive, p32-33 Shutterstock, p34 t: Gail J. Newsham archive b: Shutterstock, p35-36 Gail J. Newsham archive, p37 t: Gail J. Newsham archive b: Shutterstock, p38 t: James Boyes b: Gail J. Newsham archive, p39 Clockwise from top left: Henry Marriott Paget (1857-1936), Public domain, via Wikimedia Commons, Gail J. Newsham archive, Gail J. Newsham archive, Shutterstock, Katie Chan, CC BY-SA 4.0 <https://creativecommons.org/licenses/by-sa/4.0>, via Wikimedia Commons, Pixabay, Shutterstock, p42-43 all images Gail J. Newsham archive

Dear Reader,

As a young girl growing up in Preston, all I ever wanted to do was play football, and was always out having a kick about in the street or on the park. But, when I was your age, girls weren't allowed to play at school or have a girls' team of their own. I didn't know there had been a ban on women playing football – I just knew we couldn't play, and knew it wasn't fair.

ME!

Many years later, I discovered the story of the Dick, Kerr Ladies football team, and couldn't believe that their amazing history had been forgotten for so long. The Dick, Kerr Ladies were one of the most important teams in the history of football, so I made it my mission to discover everything I could about them.

I am thrilled to share this story of football's forgotten legends with you. I hope they will inspire you to never give up, no matter what obstacles are put in your way. Girls CAN play football, and they can play it extremely well.

Always follow your dreams, just like the Dick, Kerr Ladies did.

Love, Gail

# THE ORIGINS OF WOMEN'S FOOTBALL

## THE VERY EARLY DAYS

Lady Florence Dixie

More than 100 years ago, a feminist named Nettie Honeyball founded the British Ladies Football Club. It was 1894, and although medical professionals thought differently, Nettie saw no reason why women should not be allowed to participate in more physical sports. So Nettie advertised to find enough players, saying she was looking for women to take part in 'a manly game and show that it could be womanly as well'. But Nettie was not the only forward thinking member of the British Ladies Football Club . . . Lady Florence Dixie, whose father was the 7th Marquis of Queensberry, agreed to become president. Lady Dixie was a war correspondent for *The Morning Post* newspaper as well as a novelist, travel writer and an excellent horsewoman. It is thought she didn't play football herself – unlike Nettie, who played in defence – but she was a great supporter of women's rights.

## THE FIRST BRITISH LADIES MATCH

On March 23, 1895, around **10,000** people gathered at the Nightingale Lane ground in London, to watch the first British Ladies Football Club match. Because the players were mainly from London and the suburbs, they were divided into North and South, depending on which side of the River Thames they lived. Emma Clarke, thought to be the first black female footballer to be named in the UK, played for the South. The North scored five goals in quick succession and thrashed the South **7–1**. Although the footballing skills of both teams left a lot to be desired, they did show a great deal of enthusiasm for the game, even though they were reported to have forgotten the rules and didn't change ends at half-time!

They practised twice a week!

# WHAT DID THE PAPERS SAY?

Most of those who reported on the match did not really approve of women playing football. A reporter from the *Daily Sketch* said, 'It must be clear to everybody that girls are totally unfitted for the rough work of the football field.' And a female correspondent writing in *The Manchester Guardian* said, 'When the novelty has worn off, I do not think that women's football will attract the crowds.' Despite the harsh criticism, other matches were arranged by Lady Dixie, including a tour in Scotland and Ireland. But when a lack of finances forced the club into decline, women's football would have to wait until the outbreak of World War One before it would flourish again.

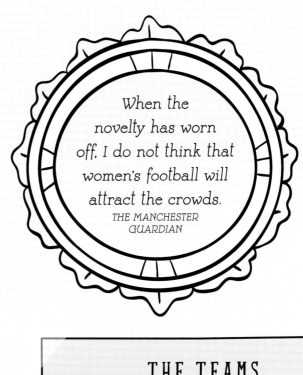

When the novelty has worn off, I do not think that women's football will attract the crowds.
THE MANCHESTER GUARDIAN

## THE TEAMS

The North

The South

# WELCOME TO THE FACTORY

## DICK, KERR & CO.

Scottish firm Dick, Kerr and Company, named for its founders, William Bruce Dick and John Kerr, set up in Preston, England in 1898. They bought a disused factory on Strand Road, then built another huge factory on the opposite side of the road, which opened in 1900. The new factory was christened 'West Works', with the other known as 'East Works' so people knew which was which. West Works was an enormous building, almost the length of three football pitches!

Hard at work in the Dick, Kerr & Co. factory

My dad and brothers all worked for Dick, Kerr.

*The industrial life of Preston has strengthened.*
THE LANCASHIRE DAILY POST, 1903

STRAND ROAD, 1910.
(Left: West Works;
Right: East Works)

*Building tramcars at Dick, Kerr & Co.*

Dick, Kerr & Co. built trams in East Works and electrical equipment for power stations in West Works, among other things. They made electric carriages for the Waterloo and City Line, one of London's first underground railways, and were responsible for electrifying 37 kilometres of the railway from Liverpool to Stockport. Replacing the old steam trains with electric made travel quicker and more reliable.

## DICK, KERR AND PRESTON

The company was one of the leading employers in the local town of Preston, providing work for many men throughout Lancashire. Dick, Kerr trams were exported worldwide, with some still in working order to this very day, and people in Preston were very proud of their factories. Because the work at Dick, Kerr was physically tough, the workforce was mostly male. But when World War One broke out in 1914 and the company was converted into a factory to make ammunition called 'shells', lots of women came to work there when the men went off to fight. The first batch of shells was made in 1915 and eventually Dick, Kerr were making **30,000** a week to help the war effort. By the end of the war in 1918, a staggering total of **3,300,000** shells had been produced. In 1919, Dick, Kerr & Co. became part of the newly founded English Electric Company and went from strength to strength, providing much-needed jobs for the people of Preston.

AUGUST 4, 1914

# The Daily News

## GREAT BRITAIN DECLARES WAR

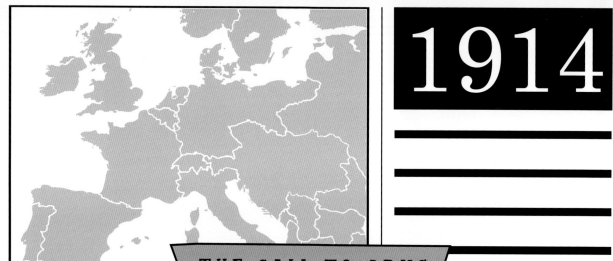

# 1914

### THE CALL TO ARMS

Britain declared war on Germany on August 4, 1914. The recruitment of soldiers that followed took place all over the country as every fit man between the age of 18 and 41 was needed to fight. There was no shortage of applicants, and by the end of 1914, just under 1.2 million men had enlisted. Of the many who said goodbye to their loved ones that year, a lot of them thought going to war would be an exciting adventure that would probably be over by Christmas. But there would be three more Christmasses to come after that before war was finally over.

# THE PRESTON STATION BUFFET

Preston railway station was extremely busy during World War One, with servicemen from all over the country passing through on their way to the battlefields of Europe. A free buffet was set up by a ladies' fundraising committee to provide refreshments and a place to rest for more than 3 million soldiers and sailors making the long journey to and from war. The men appreciated the 'steaming buckets of tea and coffee' and 'heaped-up baskets of food' and the volunteers received countless letters of thanks for their kindness from grateful servicemen. The buffet was open 24 hours a day with the ladies working 12-hour shifts.

*Volunteers at the station buffet*

You have no idea what a treat it was and how comfortable it made us for the rest of the journey.

The provision of gratuitous refreshments at 2.30 a.m. is undoubtedly service!

RETURN TO PRESTON STATION BUFFET
PROPERTY OF PRESTON STATION BUFFET

# THE DICK, KERR BOYS GO TO WAR

Some of the men working at the Dick, Kerr factory were in what was known as 'starred occupations', which meant that their work was needed at home to support the war effort and keep the country running. But the rest had answered the call to join the armed forces and fight. Many of the soldiers from Dick, Kerr & Co. were killed in action and never returned home. A memorial plaque was put up in Ashton Park, Preston, honouring the sacrifice these men made for their home town and their country.

# WOMEN AND WAR

## THE HIDDEN ARMY

The outbreak of war in 1914 saw millions of young men called upon to fight. No other war before this one had seen such a huge loss of life or limb, mainly due to the introduction of modern weaponry. The soldiers required a continuous supply of weapons, ammunition, food and medical supplies and the demand increased as the war continued. The Secretary of State for War, Lord Kitchener, used recruitment posters to tell men that he wanted them to join up. But the country needed women too, to help make all these vital supplies. Women became the nation's hidden army and they began to take their place in the UK's factories as fast as the men were leaving them for the war. From driving trams and carrying coal from the mines, to farming and working as mechanics, there were women in positions of employment that they would never otherwise have held. They did everything necessary to keep the country going so the nation could win the war, and the role they played was vital in achieving that aim.

## A FACTORY WORKER'S UNIFORM

Women in the factories had to wear special shoes and clothing to protect them from the dangerous chemicals they were working with. They also had to wear caps, so their hair didn't get caught in machinery, and jewellery was forbidden – even wedding rings had to be removed before starting work.

# WOMEN AT DICK, KERR & CO.

Many women from the local area volunteered to work at Dick, Kerr & Co. during the war. These women had loved ones who had enlisted and would have been constantly worried about them, waiting for letters to arrive with news, but they still rolled up their sleeves and got to work while supporting one another and keeping up morale. A source from the time says that around two thousand women were employed at one time by Dick, Kerr & Co.

A munitions worker's badge

## MUNITIONETTES

'Munitions' is a shortened word for ammunition, and the women who worked in factories like Dick, Kerr became known as munitionettes. They were exposed to dirty and dangerous conditions, were expected to work extremely long hours and regularly put their lives on the line. Munitionettes working on overhead cranes saw a number of fatal accidents, and those working in the aircraft industry could be severely harmed by the highly toxic chemicals used to waterproof the aircraft, suffering side effects like headaches, nausea, fainting and sometimes even death. But the most visible side effect of munitions work was seen in those women who had the task of filling shells with T.N.T. This highly explosive chemical caused the hair and skin of the workers to turn yellow, and this became known as 'toxic jaundice'. Women who were affected by T.N.T. poisoning were nicknamed 'canaries', after the bright yellow bird of the same name. And as with all explosives, they could sometimes go off unexpectedly, causing facial injuries and loss of eyes and fingers – injuries which could end up being fatal.

*A munitionette fills a shell at Dick, Kerr & Co., c.1915*

# MOOR PARK MILITARY HOSPITAL

Nurses and patients at Moor Park hospital, 1916

 ## TREATING THE WOUNDED

Preston's Moor Park Military Hospital was established in January 1915 to look after soldiers who had been injured in the war. It started off as a single wooden building in the park with only 40 beds, but was extended several times to eventually include an operating theatre and almost seven times as many beds. The hospital quickly gained a reputation as one of the leading military hospitals in the UK, and among the more than 3200 wounded soldiers treated there were at least seventy casualties from the Battle of the Somme who arrived in September 1916. When war was over, many locals and staff protested the hospital's closure as the need for its services hadn't ended, but it eventually had to shut its doors in early 1919.

Not a single girl wished to leave and we are all devoted to the place and our work.
– VOLUNTEER NURSE ERMYNTRUDE DE TRAFFORD

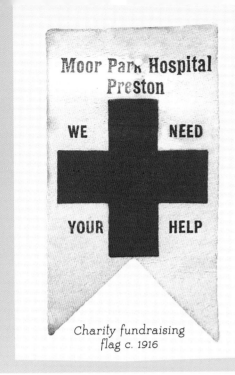

*Charity fundraising flag c. 1916*

## THE DICK, KERR LADIES CHARITY MATCH

There was no NHS in the UK at this time, and as the hospital continued to grow, money was desperately needed to keep it going. In 1917, the matron of Moor Park contacted Dick, Kerr & Co. to ask for help. She suggested a charity concert, but the factory girls thought it would be more exciting to play a ladies' football match instead. A team was chosen after around 200 women working in the factory came to trials and the game was played on Christmas Day, 1917 at Deepdale, the home of Preston North End football club.

## THE LANCASHIRE DAILY POST
# MATCH REPORT

There were 10,000 people at Deepdale yesterday afternoon at the ladies football match between the munition workers of Dick, Kerr's and Coulthard's Foundry. It was the biggest crowd that has been seen this year. After their Christmas dinner, the majority no doubt went with the object of being amused by this distinctly war-time novelty, but all agreed at the end that the quality of football shown was much better than they had expected. Within five minutes Dick, Kerr's had scored through Miss Whittle, and before half time they added further goals by Miss Berkins, a fine shot from fifteen yards out, and Miss Rance. Coulthard's, who were quite out of the picture in the first half, 'bucked up' after the interval, and deserved a goal, but it was denied them, much to the disappointment of the spectators. On the other hand, Dick, Kerr's added to their score, Miss Rance running through and netting whilst the backs were arguing about some alleged offence. The result being a 4-0 victory to the Dick, Kerr Ladies with £600 being raised for the Moor Park Hospital.

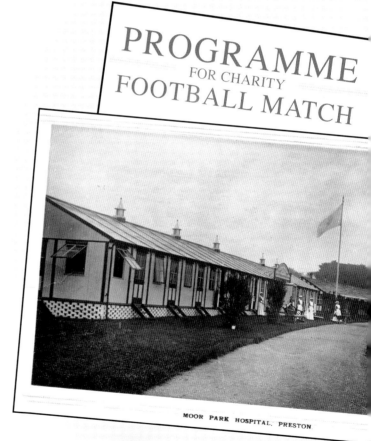

# PROGRAMME
### FOR CHARITY
# FOOTBALL MATCH

MOOR PARK HOSPITAL, PRESTON

*That'd be like £50,000 in your money today!*

# FOOTBALL AT THE DICK, KERR FACTORY

## SPORT IN THE FACTORIES

Women at work at Dick, Kerr & Co., c.1915

For the more than **900,000** women now working in munitions factories, sport was actively encouraged – to help them get rid of what was seen as the excess energy and excitement that came from being employed, but also to keep them fit and healthy for work. Factories had welfare officers to keep an eye on how the munitionettes were feeling and behaving – there hadn't been such a female-heavy workforce until now, so factories were being extra careful that their new workers were able to stay well.

## WOMEN ON THE BALL

Although women had played football before, the sport took off in a big way during World War One. Teams were formed in munitions factories all over the country as more female workers began playing the game, not least the Dick, Kerr Ladies of the Strand Road factory, Preston! The players took it very seriously and enjoyed the new-found freedom of being able to competitively play a sport normally regarded as a man's game. The fundraising from matches also enabled the women to feel they were doing something to help their loved ones who were away at war.

*They are doing their bit by work; all honour to them ... They all have hearts as big as a lion.*
*MALE MUNITIONS WORKER ON FEMALE FOOTBALLERS, AUGUST 1917*

VINTAGE LEATHER FOOTBALL BOOTS

## WORK AND SPORT

The women who played for Dick, Kerr Ladies also had to make sure they were keeping up with their important factory work. Training and playing matches had to be fitted around their working day. As the team became more established, training sessions would take place during the day on Tuesdays, Wednesdays and Thursdays, so it is likely that each player would have attended training when it was their day off from the factory. Munitions work was hard enough on its own, and adding training and playing on top of that would have been extremely tiring for the girls. But, they were dedicated to their sport, their team and their charity causes.

*Our boots would get heavier when they got wet.*

## STRENGTH AND STAMINA

Captain Alice Kell told a newspaper that the Dick, Kerr Ladies coach, George Birkenshaw, trained them hard and almost as strictly as if they were a men's First Division league club. The players kept themselves in match condition by sprinting, skipping and plenty of drills with the ball. Riding a bike, doing leap-frogs and even boxing was sometimes included to keep the training varied. As Alice said, 'We can stick a fast game on a heavy ground till the sound of the whistle,' which suggests the girls worked really hard on their levels of stamina.

SPRINT TRAINING FOR THE DICK, KERR LADIES

## THE FIRST DICK, KERR LADIES TEAM

After the groundbreaking Christmas Day charity match for Moor Park Hospital, the Dick, Kerr Ladies' first eleven firmly established themselves as far more than a gang of munitionettes who joined in with the kickabouts at the factory in tea breaks and lunchtimes. Led by their captain, Alice Kell, a calm and well-respected woman, the team went on to play more charity matches. The Ladies fast became famous, much to the delight of the management at Dick, Kerr & Co., who enjoyed the free advertising for their company!

*The Dick, Kerr Team c. 1917*

*I take my football seriously!*

Come on then, girls, let's have a go!
*GRACE SIBBERT*

### GRACE SIBBERT

Without Grace Sibbert, there might never have been a Dick, Kerr Ladies team. Grace enjoyed the good-natured teasing that went on between the girls and the boys in the factory, and when the boys challenged the girls to a football game, some time before the charity game of 1917, Grace immediately took up the challenge and rallied a team together to play. Ill health prevented her from taking any further part in the team but she remained an inspiration to the other girls.

## ALICE KELL

**Place of birth**.......Preston, Lancashire
**Date of birth**.......June 24, 1898
**Height**..................5'5"
**Playing position**....Defence/right-back

## FLORRIE RANCE

**Place of birth**.......Preston, Lancashire
**Date of birth**........1894
**Height**..................5'8"
**Playing position**.....Upfront

## ELIZABETH BERKINS

**Place of birth**.......Preston, Lancashire
**Date of birth**........Unknown
**Height**..................5'3"
**Playing position**....Midfield

## LILY JONES

**Place of birth**......Preston, Lancashire
**Date of birth**.......May 24, 1893
**Height**..................5'4"
**Playing position**....Left wing/inside
forward

# THE GAFFER

Alfred Frankland worked at the Dick, Kerr factory as a clerk during World War One. Legend has it that he could see the girls playing football with the apprentices in the factory yard from the window of his office, and when they wanted to get their team together, he offered his help. Mr Frankland was

Boots and laces must always be clean!

dedicated to the team, remaining as manager of the Dick, Kerr Ladies from the very beginning, until his death in 1957. He was a very good organiser with a natural flair for promotion, and with a great deal of support from the company management, he helped spread the word about the team. Mr Frankland was strict and always expected the girls to be punctual and keep their kit clean.

# UNPACK THE KIT

## WHAT WOMEN WORE

COVERED ARMS

CORSET

LONG SKIRT

CAP

JERSEY

SHORTS

BOOTS

Women in the late nineteenth and early twentieth century generally wore long skirts or dresses with tight, restrictive corsets that drew in their waists – as Lady Dixie described it in 1895, 'straitjacket attire'. They were expected to cover their arms and legs and their hair had to be tied up. It caused quite a stir when, around the time of World War One, the female footballers began wearing the same football kit as men did, including looser, shorter shorts! Showing their legs was a bold statement, when you compare it to the corsets and skin-covering clothing women had to wear in everyday life. But it soon became the norm and ladies' teams of that era mostly wore shorts in all their games.

## ABOUT THE BALL

Footballs in the early twentieth century were usually made of brown leather, with an animal bladder on the inside to enable the ball to be inflated. The size and weight of the ball would be more or less the same as today, but on wet days the ball would get heavier as the game went on because the leather would absorb the rain water. This could make headers difficult and quite dangerous.

'The members of the (British Ladies' Football) club do not play in fashion's dress, but in knickers and blouses. They actually allow the calves of their legs to be seen, and wear caps and football boots! Terrible! is it not? "Quite too shocking!" as an old society dame remarked to me with a shudder, adding squeakily, "And I certainly should never allow dear Mynie to so demean herself!" I looked at her and "dear Mynie", whom she was chaperoning to a ball, and said nothing, though I thought a good deal. And amidst my thoughts I wondered which looked most decent, my lithe, agile football teams, in their dark blue knickers and cardinal and pale blue blouses, and this old slave of fashion and her unnaturally attired charge, with their naked shoulders and arms, pinched-in waists, high-heeled shoes and grotesque balloon-like shoulders . . . I could only come to one conclusion, and that one may be readily guessed.'

*Lady Florence Dixie,*
*writing in* The Pall Mall Gazette,
*8 February 1895*

Tut, tut, ladies wearing shorts? It's shameful! Whatever next?

## DICK, KERR KIT

It is thought that the kit worn by the Dick, Kerr Ladies in the early days of the team consisted of hand-me-downs from the factory's men's team. The girls played in black-and-white-striped shirts, light blue shorts and black-and-white socks, with white shirts worn for international matches. They had to wear hats to keep their hair tucked in as the wearing of hairgrips and pins wasn't allowed, but thanks to women like Lady Dixie speaking up, corsets were not part of the kit!

> *This financial result can only be described as magnificent, and a tribute to those who have organised the team and played in it.*
> THE LANCASHIRE DAILY POST

## WHAT MAKES A TEAM

The Dick, Kerr Ladies were raising huge sums of money by organising and playing matches, The final amount that went to war charities at the end of the 1917/18 season was almost **£805.00** which was an enormous sum of money. Despite widespread disapproval of ladies' football, *The Lancashire Daily Post* described this total as 'magnificent' in an article from August 31, 1918.

## KICKING OFF

Nine-year-old Judith Todd had the honour of kicking off the match against Bolton Ladies on March 29, 1918. Judith's mum, well known for her local charity and political work, was the original choice, but Mrs Todd thought it would be a very undignified business to stand in the middle of a football stadium and kick a ball while wearing her best clothes. Judith herself was thrilled at the prospect of wearing a pair of shorts like those worn by the Dick, Kerr Ladies, but her parents were horrified, sending her out in a navy skirt instead. Her father, knowing his daughter well, told her firmly that she was not to stay and join the game, and as Judith later remembered, she successfully kicked the ball like he'd taught her and then obediently ran back to the stands, weaving like a proper footballer around the great grown women who rushed past in pursuit of the ball.

People paid good money to watch us play!

## JENNIE HARRIS ('LITTLE JENNIE')

**Place of birth**...Lancaster, Lancashire
**Date of birth**....December 28, 1887
**Height**...............4'10"
**Playing position**....Inside forward

## JESSIE WALMSLEY

**Place of birth**....Carnforth,Lancashire
**Date of birth**.....1895
**Height**................5'8"
**Playing position**..Defence/midfield

## MOLLY WALKER

**Place of birth**......Preston, Lancashire
**Date of birth**........1899
**Height**...................5'5"
**Playing position**...Upfront/midfield

## ANNIE HASTIE

**Place of birth**......Preston, Lancashire
**Date of birth**........Unknown
**Height**...................5'5"
**Playing position**...Goalkeeper

# FLORRIE REDFORD

Born in York on January 7, 1900, Florrie Redford was considered by some, including manager Mr Frankland, to be the best female footballer in the world. Florrie mainly played at centre forward and her ability to kick the ball equally well with both feet made her a dangerous opponent for other teams to face. She played in the first Dick, Kerr Ladies match in 1917 and went on to score many crucial goals for the team – her grand total for 1921 being a staggering **170** goals! Florrie was leading scorer during the tour of USA in 1922.

# PRESTON NORTH END

## A HOME AT DEEPDALE

Deepdale, the home of Preston North End football club and for a time, the Dick, Kerr Ladies, has a long and proud history. Preston North End FC was one of the original founder members of the Football League in 1888 and are the only club still playing at the same ground they started at! When football was halted during World War One, Deepdale's stands fell silent, except for the occasional charity football or cricket match, like that played by the Dick, Kerr Ladies and Coulthard Foundry on Christmas Day, 1917. After their Christmas Day match, the Dick, Kerr Ladies were given permission by Preston North End to use Deepdale for more games, and even for their training sessions. The Ladies paid £12 to hire Deepdale for a Saturday match, £20 for a Christmas Day match and £1 for each training session. It would have meant a great deal to the girls that they could play at their local ground.

We were proud to train and play at Deepdale.

At the height of their success, the Dick, Kerr Ladies were attracting big crowds and raising impressive sums of money for charity. In 1920, they played in front of over **350,000** spectators across 31 games, and raised what would be over **£1 million** today. In 1921, it was almost **900,000** spectators across 67 games and roughly **£3 million** (in today's money) raised!

LADIES' FOOTBALL MATCH
TOWN GROUND, Park Road.
Kick off at 6 pm
*Admission 1s.*

ST. HELENS LADIES
*VERSUS*
DICK KERR'S LADIES

## PRESTON'S FINEST

Preston North End were at the top of their game in their early years as a club. They were undefeated in all their matches and won the FA Cup without conceding a single goal throughout the entire competition. They even beat one team **26–0**! Because of their enormous success, they became known as the Invincibles. One of the Invincibles, Bob Holmes, also worked at the Dick, Kerr factory and was happy to share his footballing talent and experience by coaching the girls. He even took on the job of painting the footballs white for the Dick, Kerr Ladies' night matches!

*Preston North End collector cards*

## ON THE PITCH

The Dick, Kerr Ladies played at many of the most famous football grounds in the UK. From Goodison Park (Everton) and Anfield (Liverpool), to Old Trafford (Manchester United), St James' Park (Newcastle United), Stamford Bridge (Chelsea), Elland Road (Leeds United), Windsor Park (Belfast) and Celtic Park (Celtic F.C.), the Ladies played them all! But Deepdale would always be home.

*Dick, Kerr Ladies take a shot on goal*

## ARMISTICE

After four very long years of fighting, Great Britain was jubilant as it celebrated the end of the World War One and a welcome peace descended across the nation. At 11 a.m. on the 11th day of the 11th month of 1918, the guns fell silent and hostilities ceased, after the peace treaty known as the Armistice was signed. The cost to human life of the war was devastating. It is thought that around 8.5 million soldiers died during the conflict. While people at home enjoyed the celebrations, hardly anyone was left untouched by the tragedy of war and for many, life would never be quite the same again – especially not the returning soldiers.

British soldiers enter Lille, France c. 1918

Women wave flags from their windows to greet the troops c. 1918

> At noon the mills, schools, offices and some shops closed for the day ... A group of factory girls ... drove through the town cheering.
>
> THE LANCASHIRE EVENING POST

## WOMEN'S WORK

The end of war also brought to an end the mass production of munitions, and many women were no longer needed in the factories. Some would have been kept on in other roles but others returned to their previous lives, perhaps as housewives, working as maids in big houses, or in the many cotton mills in Lancashire. There was no doubt that the war had provided women with opportunities they may not have otherwise had. The campaign to give women the right to vote celebrated partial success at the General Election of December 1918, when some women over the age of thirty were allowed to vote for the very first time. In Preston, the Dick, Kerr Ladies continued playing football and raising money for charity, even after the war.

*Female munitions worker c.1918*

## COMING BACK

Soldiers returning home needed a lot of help with coming to terms with the terrible experiences they had endured during the war. Learning to cope with life-changing injuries and the loss of their close friends were just some of the difficulties the men faced as they tried to return to a normal way of life. For many, memories of the horrors of war would haunt them forever. Dick, Kerr & Co. offered support to the families of the men from the factory who went to fight, and a relief fund was set up to help. The company also bought Ashton Park in 1919, to be used as a place of leisure by the staff. At its opening Peace Day ceremony in 1919, the park was dedicated to the memory of all 149 employees who died during the war.

### ALICE WOODS

**Place of birth**.........St Helens,
Merseyside
**Date of birth**........March 20, 1899
**Height**...................5'5"
**Playing position**...Midfield

### FLORRIE HASLAM

**Place of birth**.........Lancashire
**Date of birth**..........1901
**Height**.....................5'5"
**Playing position**......Up front/forward

### ANNIE CROZIER

**Place of birth**......Preston, Lancashire
**Date of birth**.....30 September, 1895
**Height**.................5'6"
**Playing position**...Defence/midfield
and team physiotherapist

### LILY LEE

**Place of birth**........Preston, Lancashire
**Date of birth**.......1898
**Height**...................5'3"
**Playing position**...Up front/midfield

# LILY PARR

Lily Parr was just 15 years old when she joined the Dick, Kerr Ladies in 1920. The power of her left foot was legendary, and she once broke a man's arm when taking a penalty against him! She played for the team for around **30** years and scored a total of **986** goals during her long career. Lily is the most celebrated player in the history of the Dick, Kerr Ladies and in 2002, became the first female player to be inducted into the National Football Museum Hall of Fame. In 2019, a statue dedicated to her was unveiled at the museum.

### LILY PARR

**Place of birth**........St Helens, Merseyside

**Date of birth**........April 26, 1905

**Height**..................5'10"

**Playing position**....Left-back, then left wing

She amazes the crowd wherever she goes.
*THE REPORTER, 1921*

# THE FRENCH TOUR

## CHALLENGE ACCEPTED

When the French challenged the English to meet them on the football field, the Dick, Kerr Ladies gladly stepped up to the centre circle. A tour was planned, with the French Ladies invited to England for a series of matches against Dick, Kerr Ladies to raise money for soldiers and sailors back from the war. Dick, Kerr & Co. agreed to fund the costs, and were delighted that their team would be the first to tour in such a big way.

The French Team, 1920

*The danger signal is sent out from a ladies team in Paris with a challenge to England that they should pick a team of women players to meet them on an international field.*

THE YORKSHIRE POST

## WELCOME TO ENGLAND

The French team's arrival into Preston on April 28, 1920, was one enormous party! The brass band from the factory welcomed the team's train by playing the French national anthem and the press jostled to snap the best pictures of the girls as they emerged on to English soil. French people living in Lancashire came from far and wide to welcome their countrywomen and there was a dance organised at the factory in the players' honour. Madame Milliat, the French team selector, thought the reception their hosts had shown them was remarkable.

# ALICE MILLIAT

Madame Alice Milliat was a pioneer of women's sport in France. She was president of the first women's football club in Paris, the Femina Sport Club, and was a firm believer in a woman's right to play the game. Alongside her unrivalled knowledge of football, she campaigned for the inclusion of women's athletics in the 1924 Antwerp Olympics, but the International Olympic Committee said no. So Alice just went ahead and organised her own competition, hosting **20,000** spectators at the first Women's Olympic Games in Paris in 1922, where **18** world records were broken. It was this success that led to women being allowed to compete in track and field events at the Amsterdam Olympics in 1928.

> We were simply overwhelmed with kindness.
> MADAME MILLIAT

## ON TOUR

| DATE | LOCATION | CROWD | RESULT |
|---|---|---|---|
| April 30, 1920 | Preston | 25,000 | **2 – 0** D,K Ladies |
| May 1, 1920 | Stockport | 15,000 | **5 – 2** D,K Ladies |
| May 5, 1920 | Manchester | 12,000 | **1 – 1** |
| May 6, 1920 | London | 10,000 | **2 – 1** French Ladies |

**STAR PLAYER**

### JENNIE HARRIS

Jennie's skilful play was so impressive, she was carried off the pitch on the shoulders of her adoring fans.

I may be short, but I am very fast!

# DICK, KERR GO TO FRANCE!

Leaving for France, October 1920

## THE RETURN LEG

On the October 28, 1920, the Dick, Kerr Ladies were seen off from Preston railway station by a large cheering crowd. After an overnight stop in London they eventually arrived in Calais, France, a little queasy from the choppy sea-crossing across the Channel but excited to get to Paris. The welcome was as warm for the English girls as it had been for the French team in Preston, with the French players pushing past the policemen at the station to rush and greet the Dick, Kerr Ladies. They were all very happy to see each other again and eager to get on the pitch and play more matches.

## CAUSING A STIR

The arrival of the team in France caused great excitement. While out on a sight-seeing tour in Paris, the girls were regularly stopped by people wanting their autographs, including many British soldiers still on active duty in in the city. The soldiers even bundled in for a photograph taken for the *Daily Mail* newspaper in the UK! Some servicemen travelled from different parts of Northern France, just to get a glimpse of the players. The Dick, Kerr Ladies were footballing celebrities!

> Words fail to describe how glad they all were to see our team, I cannot describe their hearty greetings, I have never seen a team get a better reception than ours did.
> MR FRANKLAND

# HONOURING THE SOLDIERS

Travelling to their matches outside of Paris, the Dick, Kerr Ladies were able to see for themselves how Northern France had been devastated by World War One – towns were in ruins; people whose houses had been destroyed by bombs were living in makeshift huts made out of oil drums; barbed wire was still littering the ground. In each of the cities that hosted matches, the girls laid wreaths to honour the soldiers that had died in the war. They even discovered the grave of a young man from Preston, which moved many of them to tears. They covered his grave in a blanket of colourful flowers in tribute.

## CARMEN POMIES

French outfield player Carmen Pomies loved Preston so much she returned in 1921 to play for the Dick, Kerr Ladies! She was a champion javelin thrower in France and was also very good at tennis, swimming and of course, football. After she returned to France, Carmen brought the Femina Sport Club on tour to the UK every year to play matches for charity. Carmen was a remarkable woman away from the football field too. When World War Two broke out, she became a heroine of the French Resistance, risking her life to make false passports to help those hunted by the Nazi Gestapo to escape.

## BACK ON TOUR

| DATE | LOCATION | CROWD | RESULT |
|---|---|---|---|
| October 31, 1920 | Paris | 22,000 | 1-1 |
| November 1, 1920 | Roubaix | 16,000 | 2-0 D,K Ladies |
| November 6, 1920 | Rouen | 10,000 | 6-0 D,K Ladies |
| November 7, 1920 | Le Havre | 14,000 | 2-0 D,K Ladies |

**STAR PLAYER**

### FLORRIE REDFORD

Florrie had a great record as striker, scoring at least four of Dick, Kerr's goals in the four matches in France (records are unclear as to who scored in the final game).

I can score just as well with my left foot as with my right!

# THE FA BAN

## DECISIONS AND RULES

The Football Association (FA) is in charge of making all decisions about how football is played in England, from children's and youth teams, right through to the professional game. The oldest football association in the world, it was formed one Monday evening in October of 1863, with the purpose of establishing a set of rules for how the game should be played. During World War One, the FA heartily welcomed and supported women playing football for charity. That, however, was soon to change...

ENGLAND

## BEFORE THE BAN

In wartime, league clubs were keen to allow female players the use of their grounds for charity matches. But after the war, when professional men's football returned, some of those involved in the game were unhappy that women were still playing and they complained to the FA. They returned to their old argument that football was too rough for females and could cause them harm, even though women – many of whom had also taken on intense manual labour in factories – had been playing very happily and safely throughout the war years. The FA eventually agreed with the complaints and on December 5, 1921, they banned women from playing at all Association grounds.

## A PUBLIC OUTCRY

Everyone involved in the women's game was shocked by the FA ban, and many letters and appeals were sent to the FA in the hope they might have a change of heart. This support for female footballers, who simply wanted to play football and raise money for charity, came from all over the country, but it didn't help. The FA were adamant: there was no place for women in football. They had made their decision and there was no turning back.

It is an attempt to suppress ladies football. Let the girls play!

In present and past seasons I have watched about thirty ladies football matches between various teams and I have met the players. I have travelled with them frequently by road and rail and I have attended the various functions to which they have been invited and I have met the the Lord Mayors and also the officials of the local charities and football clubs concerned. On all sides I have heard nothing but praise for the good work the girls are doing and the high standard of their play. The only thing I now hear from the man in the street is, "Why have the FA got their knife into girls football? What have the girls done except to raise large sums for charity and to play the game? Are their feet heavier on the turf than the men's feet?"

*A letter to the secretary of the FA, from Major Cecil Kent of the Old Westminsters Football Club*

## DICK, KERR LADIES AND THE BAN

The ban was a killer blow for women's football and many teams had no option but to give up playing. The Dick, Kerr Ladies were bitterly disappointed with the decision, especially after all the money they had raised from their games. Some of the players even felt the real reason for the ban might be that ladies' teams were drawing bigger crowds on match day than the professional men's teams! Either way, no matter the difficulties that lay ahead, they were determined to carry on. If the public still wanted to watch the Dick, Kerr Ladies play, and the charities still needed them, they would play football wherever they could. The fight back had begun.

# WHAT HAPPENED NEXT FOR THE DICK, KERR LADIES?

## NO HARM TO WOMEN!

Less than three weeks after the FA ban, the Dick, Kerr Ladies had to rearrange their fixture against Fleetwood Ladies, which should have been played at an Association ground. They played on the pitch at Ashton Park instead. Team captain Alice Kell invited local doctors to the match so they could give their opinion on whether the game was harmful or not. About twenty doctors accepted the invitation and all agreed that football was no more harmful to women than either tennis or hockey. One doctor even said, 'From what I saw, football is no more likely to cause injuries to women than a heavy day's washing'. Despite the FA ban, plenty of people still continued to turn up to watch the Dick, Kerr Ladies games.

*Talking team tactics*

## A NEW TOUR

On September 15, 1922, the Dick, Kerr Ladies set sail for an adventure of a lifetime when they crossed the Atlantic to take part in a football tour. Matches had been arranged in Canada and the USA and they didn't expect to return home until 1923. But on their arrival in Quebec, the team were shocked to learn that the Canadian FA weren't going to let them play! The only alternative was to play against men's teams in the USA. The Ladies were very disappointed but decided to make the best of their time on tour and approached these games as an experiment. Out of nine games, they won three, drew three and lost three. The teams they played were some of the best men's teams in the United States.

> *The FA don't think we ought to go and tried to stop us, but failed.*
> ALICE KELL

*Dick, Kerr Ladies team photo, 1925*

# CHAMPIONSHIP OF THE WORLD

*Training hard!*

World Championship medal

By 1937, the Dick, Kerr Ladies firmly believed that they were the best women's football team in the world. But there were some who didn't agree! Edinburgh Ladies regarded themselves as the best in Scotland, and as the two teams had never met, they challenged the Dick, Kerr Ladies to a game to decide who had the right to be called world champions. Lots of newspapers took notice and turned up to Dick, Kerr training sessions to take photos, calling the forthcoming game the 'Championship of the World Match'. After a lot of hard training, Dick, Kerr Ladies won the game 5–1, with one of their goals scored by Joan Whalley, who was only 15 years old! The players all received a gold medal in honour of their victory.

# A FOOTBALLING LEGACY

*We advertised . . .
and a few girls came along
but they would never have
made footballers if they had
played till they were 90!
So we didn't really have
any alternative.*

KATH LATHAM

## THE GRAND TOTAL

In 1965, nearly fifty years after they began playing, the Dick, Kerr Ladies football team was forced to close. The manager at the time, Kath Latham, had found it hard to find enough players who were good enough to play, and she didn't want to tarnish the team's reputation by cancelling games. It was a difficult decision to make, but everyone involved could be extremely proud of what the Dick, Kerr Ladies had achieved over the years, not least what they had done for charity. Between 1917 and 1965, they had raised over **£10 million** in today's money!

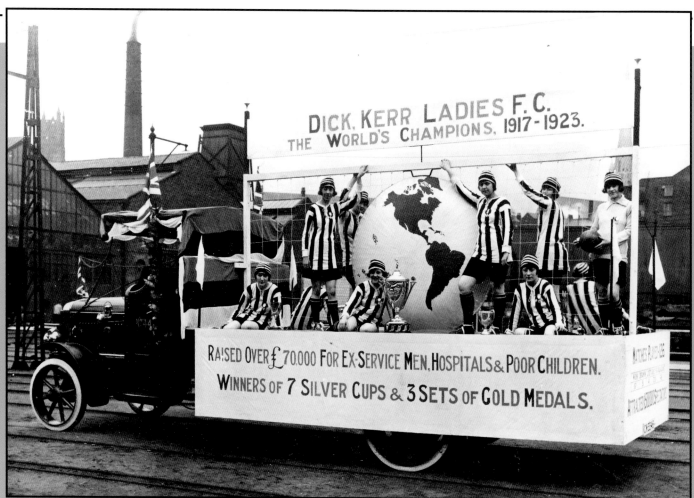

*Blackpool Carnival float, 1923*

# A FIRST IN THE WORLD FOR THE BEST IN THE WORLD

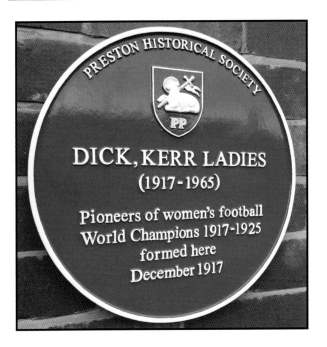

PRESTON HISTORICAL SOCIETY

PP

**DICK, KERR LADIES**
**(1917-1965)**

Pioneers of women's football
World Champions 1917-1925
formed here
December 1917

To mark **100 years** since the Dick, Kerr Ladies football team was founded in 1917, a blue plaque – a commemoration of important people and places in history – was unveiled at the site of the original Dick, Kerr factory. History was made that day, as this was the first ever blue plaque dedicated to women's football! Grandchildren of two of the original pioneers of the team, Grace Sibbert and Alice Kell, were invited to unveil the plaque at the very building where their grandmothers had worked during the war. It was recognition at last for the players who blazed a trail for women's football, against all the odds.

## PROFESSIONAL PLAYERS

When the Dick, Kerr Ladies played their first charity match on Christmas Day, 1917, they probably wouldn't have dared believe that women would play football professionally one day. But, thanks to these courageous players who worked hard to change minds and attitudes about women in sport, female footballers can now earn a living playing the game for professional teams all over the world. Women are able to represent their country at the highest level in football too, as England's 'Lionesses' team demonstrated most recently in 2019, being narrowly beaten in the World Cup semi-final by the eventual winners of the tournament, the USA. Maybe one day soon, the Lionesses will follow in the bootsteps of the Dick, Kerr Ladies of 1937, and be crowned Champions of the World!

England player Demi Stokes, 2014

THE LIONESSES TEAM, 2019

## 1895

First match played by the British Ladies Football Club.

## 1917

The Dick, Kerr Ladies football team is formed. 10,000 spectators come to Deepdale to watch them play.

## 1921

The FA bans women's football.

## 1969

The Women's Football Association is formed, with 44 member clubs.

## 2019

England reach the semi-finals of the Women's World Cup. They lose to the USA 1–2.

## 1998

Hope Powell is appointed as the first ever full-time coach of the England women's football team.

## 2014

ENGLAND

The first time the England women's team play an international match at Wembley stadium, against Germany.

# INDEX

FIRST MATCH AGAINST COULTHARD'S AT DEEPDALE Dec 1917
WON 5-0
£600 TAKEN AT THE TURNSTILES WITH A 6d GATE

FOUNDER, MANAGER & SECRETARY Mr ALFRED FRANKLAND REPUTED TO HAVE MANAGED WOMEN FOR 20 YEARS WITHOUT A CROSS WORD.

PLAYED 56 MATCHES IN ONE SEASON AND TOOK £7000 IN 3 GAMES AT LIVERPOOL MANR...

WINNERS OF 14 SILVER CUPS 6 WON OUTRIGHT) AND OF MEDALS

Sixième Année - F° 559. N° 18.    NOUVELLE SÉRIE : 18.    Le Numéro : 50 Centimes.    ÉTRANGER : 60 Cent.    Jeudi 4 Novembre 1920.

# LE MIROIR DES SPORTS

PUBLICATION HEBDOMADAIRE ILLUSTRÉE, 18, RUE D'ENGHIEN, PARIS

Abonnements : 1 An. 25 fr. 6 Mois. 13 fr.    Abonnements : 1 An. 35 fr. 6 Mois. 13 fr.

UNE JOUEUSE ANGLAISE, LYONS, SHOOTE AU COURS DU MATCH FÉMININ FRANCO-ANGLAIS DE FOOTBALL
La première partie de football, jouée en France entre deux équipes féminines anglaise et française, a eu lieu dimanche dernier au Stade Pershing et s'est terminée par un match nul : 1 but à 1. Elle fut disputée...

## Football at St. Andrews!

### PROGRAMME
:: OF ::
FOOTBALL MATCH

## DICK KERR LADIES
v.
## COVENTRY CITY LADIES

THURSDAY, 25th AUGUST, 1921,
KICK OFF 6-30 p.m.

Proceeds divided between Queen's Hospital, Birmingham, and Birmingham Boys' and Girls' Union

## 'ENTENTE CORDIALE'
### LADIES' INTERNATIONAL FOOTBALL MATCH

# ENGLAND
(DICK KERR'S OF PRESTON)
versus
# FRANCE
(LADIES OF PARIS)

## AT BROUGH PARK, NEWCASTLE
THURSDAY, 15th JULY - KICK-OFF 7.15

in aid of
Gateshead Youth Stadium Appeal Fund and
Carlisle United (New Stand) Appeal Fund

## Ladies' Football Charity Match

# PRESTON LADIES' XI
(DICK KERR'S)
versus
# BLACKPOOL LADIES' XI

## LOWER LANE GROUND, FRECKLETON
## MONDAY, JUNE 20th 1949

7-0 p.m. Laying Wreath on Memorial Grave in Churchyard

7-30 p.m. KICK-OFF
Seats Provided.

# ADMISSION 1/-

FRECKLETON PRIZE BRASS BAND
(Bandmaster: Mr. Prosser)

# WANT TO READ MORE ABOUT THE DICK, KERR LADIES?

## Try this fantastic fiction series inspired by their story.

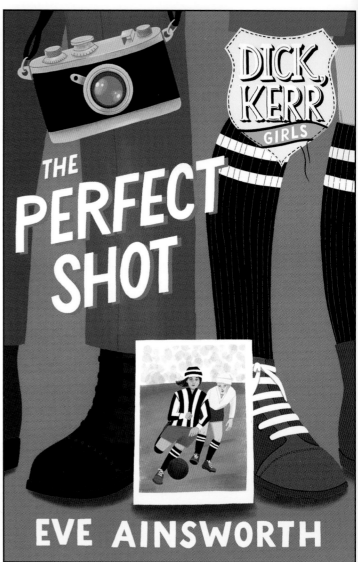

## FOR MORE INFORMATION VISIT:

www.uclanpublishing.com

uclanpublishing